The Seven Beagles of Christmas

Kellie Wynn

ISBN-13: 979-8-8659-0133-4

DEDICATION

To my inspirations - Moo Moo, Daisy Doos, and Pepper Potts, I love you to the moon and back.

CONTENTS

ACKNOWLEDGMENTS

Thank you to my darling hubby for all your help and support in everything I do.

1: THE MAGIC BEGINS

In homes adorned with twinkling lights and the sweet sound of carols, the magic of Christmas was brewing. Santa Claus, with his jolly smile, decided this year, seven beagles who needed homes would find their forever families. He knew just the families who needed a sprinkle of floppy ears and waggy tails to make their Christmas unforgettable. With a twinkle of his eyes and a wave of his magical staff, he sent the beagles on a journey of love, lessons, and laughter.

2: DAISY'S DAY WITH THE JOHNSONS

The Johnsons were finishing up their Christmas decorations when Daisy, a gentle beagle, arrived. They gave her space, resisting the urge to crowd around. Slowly, Daisy explored and eventually nestled beside Mr. Johnson. He gently patted her head, teaching: Ease in: When a new beagle arrives, give her time to settle and let her come to you when she's ready. Don't crowd her, patience is key.

3: PEPPER'S PLAYTIME WITH THE MARTINS

As snowflakes danced in the morning breeze, the Martins welcomed Pepper, a spirited beagle. They were excited, arranging cozy beds and toys. During naptime, Pepper snuggled into her bed. Little Jake, excited, tried to cuddle but Pepper growled gently. Mrs. Martin explained, "Pepper needs her rest, Jake." Understanding dawned, and Jake learned: Allow rest: Let your beagle sleep undisturbed, respecting her rest time.

4: LOIS' LESSON WITH THE HARPERS

The Harpers were a lively bunch, always playing and laughing. When Lois, a playful beagle, joined them, little Ben was overjoyed. He playfully tugged at Lois' ears and tail, but Lois yelped. Mrs. Harper said, "We must be gentle with Lois, Ben." And Ben learned: Gentle play: Play gently, avoiding tugging on ears or tails for a happy beagle.

5: BILLY'S BOUNDARIES WITH THE FLETCHERS

The Fletchers were having a quiet afternoon when Billy, a curious beagle, trotted in. He found a cozy corner and curled up in his crate. When little Sarah tried to join him, Billy barked. Mr. Fletcher said, "Billy's crate is his own little home, Sarah." Sarah nodded, learning: Crate comfort: Respect your beagle's crate as his private space, keeping it disturbance-free.

6: MOLLY'S MOMENT WITH THE ANDREWS

The Andrews were tidying up for Christmas when Molly, a playful beagle, wandered in. She quickly found a doll and started nibbling. Mrs. Andrews exchanged the doll with a tasty treat, teaching: Tidy spaces and resource guarding: Keep toys and food out of reach to ensure a safe home, and always get an adult to exchange a toy for a food treat.

7: YALA'S YUMMY FOOD WITH THE GRAYS

The Grays were setting up their Christmas lights when Yala, a shy beagle, arrived. As they sat down for dinner, little Timmy reached to pet Yala who was nibbling her kibble. But Yala growled softly. Mrs. Gray explained, "Yala needs her space while eating, love." Timmy nodded, learning the lesson: Respect mealtime: Avoid disturbing your beagle while she's enjoying her food.

8: DENNIS' DOOR WITH THE WILLIAMS

The Williams were singing carols when Dennis, an adventurous beagle, pranced in. During the joyous chaos, the front door was left ajar, and Dennis sprinted towards it. Mr. Williams swiftly closed the door, teaching: Secure boundaries: Ensure doors are closed to keep your curious beagle safe indoors.

9: CHRISTMAS DAY

As Christmas dawned, each family found joy and learned valuable lessons from their new furry members. The laughter, barks, and wagging tails echoed through the crisp winter air, creating a feeling of love and companionship that warmed every heart. The magic of Christmas, intertwined with the love for the beagles, left the families with cherished memories and joyful hearts, celebrating the true spirit of Christmas.

ABOUT THE AUTHOR

Kellie Wynn is a beagle behaviour specialist from Guernsey in the Channel Islands. Owner of adorable beagles Daisy and Pepper, Kellie's journey began with the challenges and joys they brought into her life. With a profound understanding of dog behaviour and psychology, Kellie became "The Beagle Lady." Her mission? To debunk myths surrounding beagles' temperament and to guide fellow beagle enthusiasts on a joyous journey of understanding and bonding with these beautiful animals.

www.thebeaglelady.com
kellie@thebeaglelady.com

Made in the USA
Columbia, SC
27 December 2024